T0128239

AWAKENING TO GOD

THE LIFELONG JOURNEY OF A SPIRITUAL HEALER

HELEN NELSON

authorHOUSE®

AuthorHouse™
1663 Liberty Drive
Bloomington, IN 47403
www.authorhouse.com
Phone: 1 (800) 839-8640

Published by AuthorHouse 11/19/2015

ISBN: 978-1-5049-6367-1 (sc)
ISBN: 978-1-5049-6366-4 (hc)
ISBN: 978-1-5049-6377-0 (e)

Library of Congress Control Number: 2015919345

Print information available on the last page.

This book is printed on acid-free paper.

CONTENTS

CONTENTS

Helen

Helen's father told her she was stolen from the Gypsies

A true Gypsy in her spirit......she ran wild and untamed

But as Helen she would run barefoot

Because her spirit was searching and

In her struggle to find Elu

She could only choose the difficult way.

The dark haired, green-eyed, woman-child

Who didn't believe in her beauty

Who wasn't like anyone else

Chaffed at her uniqueness

Her Gypsy spirit always struggled to be free

From the bonds of expectation and propriety

Then after the experience of death

When her new life began to emerge

She left the confines of oppressive self awareness

She shed the many layers that prevented the Gypsy spirit from

shining through,

And looked to others with the love, compassion, and gentleness

that she had always sought to receive

And her works became healing words

And her touch, a healing touch

To die and be reborn.....

For Helen it meant becoming

For the daughter, wife, mother that she was

It meant becoming finally,

Elu.

Diane Olson (11/95)

(Helen's daughter)

Chapter I

MY FIRST BRUSH WITH DEATH

It was a beautiful, sunny day in late September and the landscape was ablaze with shimmering colors of yellow, orange, red, brown and gold. The trees were like a decoupage that only God could create. The sky was filled with billowy, white clouds.

Andy and Elu

I was about five and a half years old. My younger brother, Andrew, and I were gingerly walking across the meadow, excited about soon being able to help our brother, Johnny, and our father pick apples. Andy was all snuggled into a brown jacket and I was wearing a new, bright red coat with a little fur collar and cuffs that my sister had sent from New York. Andy was teasing me by tickling me with the long, dry, blades of grasses and small branches. We laughed and laughed at the joy of the morning and the adventure. Suddenly we heard the thundering hooves of our horse, Danny, as he came upon us from behind. Andy yelled, "Elu, Elu, run, run!" (Elunka is my Hungarian name, Elu for short.) Andy's little legs carried him so fast but I turned and just stood unmoving, frozen in fear! My fear was such that I was in horror. Our family horse suddenly ran to me, grabbed hold of the neck of my new coat with his teeth and threw me over him. I landed on the ground with a *thud* and was knocked unconscious. That was all I remembered until I was told everything that happened later.

As Elu lay on the ground one of Danny's hooves came down and injured her chest. Andy yelled, "Help, help, Elu has been hurt!" She was lying on the ground bleeding from a gash in her forehead.

Her mother was horrified, as she saw this happen from the kitchen window. She went to the door and stepped outside but saw Johnny running for Elu so went back indoors to get three quilts which she laid over the huge wooden table my father had built for us. It was now prepared for Elu.

Johnny ran, gently picked up Elu's limp body and, with her father and Andy close behind, carried her up the hill into the house and, with tears in his eyes, laid her on the table. Her mother quickly but gently removed her coat and found, to her horror, that Elu was barely breathing. Mamom (Mama) gently removed Elu's coat which was spattered in blood. She noticed there were bruises on her neck, shoulders and face. Oh, mamom could barely keep from sobbing. This beautiful day which was to be so delightful for the children had turned into such a tragedy! How? Why did this happen? This beautiful mamom who had learned how to heal from her mother when she was just a child in Hungary, remembered the days and weeks her mother would teach her to heal, to pray while she was healing, and how to *become an instrument of God while doing the healing. With a family now of nine, she remembered it SO well.*

She began praying over Elu in Hungarian, while working. Andy, Johnny and papom (papa) were now there and joined in the prayers as she continued to work long and hard. She cried, "My angel child! God, please don't take my precious angel child from me!" In between prayers, she kept saying, "Elu, Elu, it is not your time, you have much work to do!" More work, more prayers. She moved her hands skillfully over Elu's whole body and when she removed some of her clothing she was horrified to see the lacerations. Mamom could tell Elu had several fractured ribs and could see there was much trauma. She could tell the pain would be almost unbearable if Elu were conscious. Her hands never stopped working. She said to papom, Johnny and Andy, "Pray, pray, pray!" Mamom prayed, "Oh God, she has the same abilities I have. Please, if it is Your will, let her live!"

Everyone heard Ethel and Anna returning so papom went outdoors to tell them what had happened and asked them to be as quiet as possible upon entering the kitchen. When they came in they both began to cry, then joined in the prayers while papom somehow did all the things he needed to do as a very competent father. Every so often he would put his arms around mamom to encourage her. He would say, "Rest, edes (sweet) asszony" (woman). He brought her a chair so she could still run her hands from Elu's head to her toes, over and over again while sitting down. Mamom asked for her rosary beads and started using them.

Johnny went out to the barn to take care of all the animals as papom felt he should take care of mamom, staying close to her to give her strength, faith and to pray with her. "Dear God, help us to understand. Help us to understand there is a reason for everything." Mamom, hearing his beautiful prayers, began to weep a little and then prayed with him.

Soon there was a lessening of the whimpering and mamom gently and intuitively skimmed her hands over Elu's body, still feeling the tremendous trauma. The room was shining with light and the heat from the old, black wood/coal stove in the kitchen began to penetrate the room. The prayers of papom, Johnny and Andy were heard. The voice of little Andy kept saying, "Elu, Elu, come back Elu." This was a place where the intensity of love and serenity was felt. They heard a little more whimpering and then soft crying. Mamom stood up and looked to see if there were any signs of healing, of renewal, and amazingly noticed that one leg moved just a little bit. She said," Oh, my God, Guri, (George) Guri, Elu is regaining consciousness!"

Slowly the whimpering became stronger and Elu gradually began to breathe normally. The pain must have been intense for this child. As Elu opened her eyes all mamom could hear was "Fáj, (pain) fáj,!" Mamom said, "I'm here, I know." Suddenly Andy appeared and asked, "Mamom, is she getting better?" Mamom said, "I hope and pray so." Papom prayed, "Dear God, please help this child and help us to help her." Mamom, who had many healing herbs drying, put a few drops of her herbal medication on Elu's lips. It was her formula for pain and wellness, which helped as their daughter very slowly regained consciousness.

It was as if I had simply been dropped onto that soft, beautiful bed that my mother had prepared for me. I felt intense pain but also love and had the feeling that everything would be all right. Even though it was difficult for me to speak I told mamom I remembered such light and such peace! "I saw angels, mamom, angels! They were so beautiful!" I had no recollection of anything at our farm after seeing Danny running toward me, only awakening in that soft bed.

By the grace of God and the strength within me that sometimes comes with suffering yet is hard to comprehend, there was a determination in me that said "I must get well." As mamom continued to work, slowly my crying stopped and the pain began to ease. Oh, this wise mother constantly thanked God for her family and somehow the sun seemed brighter and the room warmer. Johnny came in, saw that I had awakened, and knew what his mother could do, with God's help. It was way beyond the comprehension of most people, but he knew.

Each day I became stronger. The first thing I asked for was "My red coat, my red coat." Mamom told me it was right beside me. I kept talking about angels until mamom told me to be quiet and rest, that soon I would be well enough to sit up and have some homemade chicken soup. Such love surrounded me. If only more families today would recognize the love of God.

This beautiful Hungarian lady who was my mother, referred to me as a little "cigany" or little "gypsy" and continued to work on me until I fell asleep. Andy insisted on staying close to the bed and with his little hands would touch me softly and sing to me. "Get well my little Elu, get well."

In a few days my parents were able to take me to the doctor who ordered x-rays which confirmed four fractured ribs. Because of these I could hardly move but mamom said I was doing well. I asked her to sing and then listened to the beautiful Hungarian songs that she sang for me. It seemed to me that mamom could do anything.

That was the way it would go in the old farmhouse in Harwinton, Connecticut. Such an abundance of everything that was needed was there. The vegetables, eggs, milk, the cheeses and the love – it was all there. It was such a beautiful, heavenly place. Isn't it amazing how suffering makes one aware of the love, beauty and the wonder around you? This old farmhouse, surrounded by trees, birds, squirrels and so much more seemed even more delightful to me.

I remember the wide, brown floorboards in that room as well as the fireplace. Mamom would put herbs on the wood to give me a pleasant aroma to enjoy during the days. She also had a little gold bag she made and would fill it with her own mixture of potpourri.

Several weeks later when I was able to sit outdoors in the sunshine for a while my parents fixed a comfortable chair with soft pillows for me to sit on, and blankets. They placed it on the patio because of the view of such lovely scenery. The first time I looked around was an amazing sight! "I have never seen anything like this before! I said, "Oh mamom, papom, you are shining! My hands are shining! How beautiful the sun is. The sky is so blue! Something is moving around everything!" "I hear bells!" Papom laughed. "Elu, that is our cow being led to the barn. Her new bell is so we know where she is."

Helen adds now, in her own words, what her parents might have said:

Papom said, "Elu, God has given you a gift. You now see what others do not see. Sometimes it will be a joy but other times it will be a burden because others will tell you about their sadness, their loneliness, or their pain. God has given you the ability to speak to them quietly and slowly, to make them understand. It is what God calls 'awakening.' Everyone is awakening gradually but you are now beyond. You will hear things that others cannot comprehend. The music you love so much will be more beautiful, also the sounds.

The music of Nelson Eddy and Jeanette MacDonald that you enjoy
so much will now be more enjoyable than ever before."

I began to cry but mamom said, "No, Elu, do not cry." Then, suddenly I began to laugh. Mamom and papom did also at the sight of me all bundled up like a little teddy bear. Then I said again, "Everything is shining and beautiful!"

When mamom and papom helped me back into the house, they seated me in front of the old, black stove so I could get warm. They held my hands and looked at me in amazement. They may have thought:

"This child has been awakened so profoundly. Oh, my God,
will we be able to help her?" But then they realized they would
not be leading, it would be God.

Papom took my hand and said, "My little darling girl, it is
going to be a tough world for you but it will also be a world of such
beauty, such awakening, such awareness that other people will not
be able to understand it. How will they see that when you look at
someone and see that something inside of them is ill or broken or

the pain is severe and you, without questioning, say to them, 'You are being healed.' You will get better, be strong." Papom looked at me and knew I did not understand. "You know, my dear, sweet little woman, you are living in a strange world. Through your suffering and trauma you have somehow been given a precious gift that is so rare, so hard to find. My little Elu, they will look to you, walk to you, and want to talk to you always, saying, "How do you know?" All you will say is, "I don't know -- only God knows." "You know, this whole world, this whole life that you are in now, that you have been born for, is to heal and to awaken people to the power of unconditional love -- the power of compassion. Oh, my little child, my little lady, God has given you such a gift. One day when I am no longer here and you are a very beautiful woman you will remember and say, 'Oh, my beautiful papom.'"

Mamom and papom realized it was impossible for me to understand what had happened or what would continue to happen. Mamom and papom reached for each other, holding hands, tears running from their eyes, and prayed for direction and knowledge in healing and raising me. Papom looked at me and said, "Look out world, here she comes. The little cigany that always ran barefoot through the woods, listening to the whispers of the trees - here she is, that wild, little cigany woman, so awake, so alive that nothing will be able to put her back to sleep. There is so much that has to be changed in her world, in our world." Then my father bowed his head and prayed, "This little severely injured child, oh God, I am so honored to be her father. Help me to be a wise, intelligent father and speak to her with wisdom, compassion and the unconditional love of the God within her and the God within everyone."

This was my first brush with death. I knew everything would be alright because of the love around me. My dear mother knew I would never forget as she cared for me through my extremely painful but full recuperation.

Chapter II

MY HUNGARIAN FAMILY

My parents came to America from Hungary where my mother, Julianna, learned to heal from her mother. She had recognized my healing abilities even before my injury from our horse, Danny, but could tell that now my abilities were stronger. If someone in our family had been burned, she would call me to help her. She was continually teaching me.

We lived on the farm in Harwinton but my mother was a healer who went wherever she was needed. She was known as the beautiful healer who would walk miles to heal, help the dying and aid in the delivery of babies.

When I was a little older she took me with her on her visits. She would tell me to stop, be still, watch, listen and pay close attention to everything she said and did. But at this time I just thought it was exciting to go here and there with my mother as

I did not realize I had an ability to heal. As I grew older I could run my hands over the body and feel the cancer, the disorders of other kinds, and would be fascinated.

Sometimes we would take the bus to the area of Torrington I called the "Hungarian Village" because mamom had many friends there whom we would visit. My mother would carry her big satchel filled with containers of her homemade cottage cheese to give to needy families. I heard fascinating stories about Old Hungary and the wonders of that country. Those were always special days.

I was loved and cherished by my parents and siblings so had a beautiful childhood on our farm. My sisters teased and sometimes called me "Little Elu." I was the eighth of nine children, four boys and five girls and was born in Hebron, Connecticut during one of the state's most powerful blizzards. There was neither a way to get a mid-wife to come nor to get my mother to the hospital in that weather so my father was the one who lovingly aided my mother in the delivery, with much prayer, and cut the cord. He then looked at her with great love in his eyes, wrapped me in a blanket and placed me in her waiting arms, looked at me and said, "Igy szep, igy edes!"

("So beautiful, so sweet!") He held my mother and lovingly cared for both of us. Being a clergyman, he baptized me the following day.

****

Our family was not well off financially but we learned to be thrifty, creative, disciplined, and were happy with what we had. Living in a large family meant that people seemed to be going somewhere or doing something special all the time. It seemed as if I was saying "Me too" much of the time so "Me too" became my nickname.

I enjoyed jumping from high places so my mother was always repairing my injuries. One day she said, "Elu, why do you jump from such high places?" I said, "Because I am carried by angels!"

My father was from Budapest and was artistic and creative in many ways. He was the first of our family to come to America. He came to find a place for his family to live and we moved several times before settling on the farm in Harwinton.

Both of my parents and all of the children worked very hard. My mother was a marvelous cook and when she made a huge pot of chicken soup she always used two chickens, carrots, parsley and many other vegetables and spices. It had to feed many people but oh, how we enjoyed it. Andy and I always sat next to each other and papom sat at the head of the table.

When we had a regular chicken dinner, however, being next to the youngest in the family meant I would get the neck of the chicken and Andy would get the wing. To this day I will not eat the neck of the chicken. Papom would get white meat, Johnny would get a thigh and leg. Ethel would get some white meat and Anna would get a thigh.

My getting the neck of the chicken combined with two other events. The first was that I rode in the rumble seat of my sister's car when she would treat me to a ride on a weekend, making me feel like a queen. The second was that our family umbrellas were handed down. With my father, brothers and sisters working, by the time one was handed down to me it always leaked. One night at the dinner table I got the neck of the chicken again and felt like crying but said, "No!" I suddenly made up this song and sang it at the table:

I get the neck of the chicken,

I get the rumble seat ride.

I get the leaky umbrella,

I'm so happy to be alive!

Everyone clapped and laughed. They thought it was so funny! Indeed we were a happy family.

In the winter many times we would come indoors after a long time in the snow and remove our boots, hats and mittens and crowd around the old, black kitchen stove to warm up. Mamom smiled as she always did, looking at her children with such love and gratitude. She wondered often about my remarks after my trauma. Sometimes papom would play his violin in the kitchen and mamom would cry from happiness. The wood crackled and we would make popcorn on cold nights. If we needed extra ice for some reason in the winter we would put a container of water on the windowsill at night and in the morning it would be a container of ice.

Such a wondrous life and family. So much love, laughter and joy. Somehow my Hungarian mamom was so gracious. There was an aura of beauty in that old, leaky farmhouse. The love, the awareness and kindness to each other. The love and compassion of my mamom and papom. Many stories of Hungary, about Budapest. The reverence for God was always present, even on the darkest, coldest, rainiest days. Always that presence of love, dignity, beauty and such gratitude! To be in this beautiful country! My mamom and apom felt it such an honor to be here. The love that pervaded that home, that farm, that era. How blessed we were!

SUMMER MORNING

Capriciously the willows whisper

in the morning mist

as glistening leaves

caress the limpid pool

and azure brush strokes

plummet to mysterious depths

painting Grecian splendor.

Pine and birch, reflecting mirrored images

and clouds, proudly

present vistas of alabaster forms.

The perch and minnow leap in spraying joy

to catch the idle insect

while the queenly frog

sits sedately on her lily pad

arrumping eloquent commands.

Dew kissed blades of grass

bend with crystalline heaviness,

hinting of a separate universe

clothed in mystic wonder.

Now, the iridescent butterfly with majestic wings,

alights on stately iris

elegantly robed in indigo hues.

Kaleidoscopic sound and color blend,

creating pastoral bliss and universal lyre

while blessedly

this paradise sustains our souls

as reverently we touch our God each day.

Helen Lucas Nelson

1979

Chapter III
HOLIDAYS AND SPIRITUAL GIFTS

Christmas was very different than it is now. Because we did not have much financially we learned to be happy with little. I would draw poinsettias with chalk. Andy and I would go into the forest with our brother John. I remember this very special holiday season when we had an exhilarating day. The sky was a vivid, bright blue. The sun was sparkling and shining on the snow flakes that had recently touched the tree branches and the ground. Dear, dear Johnny brought out the old, beat up toboggan, tied a rope around it, then tied the rope around his waist. Andy and I were almost trembling with joy and the excitement of the adventure. I, somehow, by the grace of God, had overcome my physical and emotional trauma from the tragedy I had undergone with the accident from our horse, Danny. It was now forgotten and it seemed almost as if I had come back from that with a greater joy -- a greater zest for life! I found everything more beautiful, brighter and more delightful. Somehow that painful episode in the fall had truly increased my awareness of beauty. Andy was always by my side like a little guard, watching over me. Johnny was smiling so much for our joy. Perhaps he remembered when he was a little boy.

Andy and I jumped onto the toboggan. We were small and very light. Our dog, Boots, ran and jumped beside us, wagging his tail. He had been named Boots because of the white that went partially up his forelegs. He also had a bushy, white tail. I was in awe of the light casting shadows on the fields, the branches, and the grass. It was as if I had never seen them before.

As we went on, Johnny, in his beautiful voice, sang "Santa Claus is Coming to Town" to us as we laughed and clapped our hands. Across the meadow and frozen brook we went and then came to the area where the corn had grown in the summer. It was harder for Johnny to pull there as it was uphill so Andy and I got off the toboggan. We ran, slid and enjoyed ourselves but when we came to the opening of the meadow and the forest we stepped over some logs and were quiet so as not to disturb the cows. As we entered the forest Johnny said, "Listen -- the birds are singing. They know that Christmas is coming. Listen to the trees -- if you listen really, really hard you can hear them whispering to each other! Did you know that when one falls in a storm the others will pick it up?" He smiled a little bit after *that* story! Andy and I were laughing at the breaths of steam coming from our nostrils. I said, "Look, Johnny, I'm smoking a cigarette!"

As we entered the forest it was magnificent. The sun shone brightly between the tree branches with a glow I had never noticed before. You could hear the branches brush against each other. Johnny would say, "Be quiet so you can hear the winter birds sing and the little animals, perhaps even a fox. It is important to be quiet in the forest as we look for our tree." But being young, Andy quickly said, "Look! Rabbits!," as several crossed our paths. Suddenly Andy and I were so excited we clapped our hands and laughed, singing, "Jingle Bells, Jingle Bells ...." So much for quiet! Dear Johnny actually had tears in his eyes, no doubt so grateful I was alive to enjoy another Christmas. Perhaps he was also remembering his childhood.

Johnny stopped to pick some laurel. The branches of the shrubs were elegant in the house during the winter months.

Then we went on to the task of choosing our tree. Johnny said it could not be too tall, too short, too skinny or too fat. Andy and I laughed. Suddenly the sun poured down in a magnificent cylinder of light that shone on the snow in a spot close to us. It felt to me as if I were in a cathedral! There was also a tree close by that looked lovely. I said, "Look, Andy, what do you think?" Johnny looked also and said he did not think it would fit in the living room because it was too tall. As they walked by I touched one of its branches as if I wanted to say, "How beautiful you are."

In a little while Andy said, "Look, Johnny, that tree is about as big as you are. Not too tall, too short or too fat!" We all agreed and Johnny took out his small ax to cut the tree down and suddenly I began to cry. Johnny said, "Elu, why are you crying?" I said, "Oh Johnny, you will hurt the tree if you cut it down!" Johnny said, "Oh Elu, I know how to chop very gently so as not to hurt it and in two more winters there will be another just like it. The roots are still there -– nothing ever dies." That seemed to somehow subdue me a little as I was so aware of life around me. Johnny looked up and said, "I think we should say a prayer to God for this beautiful little tree and also the forest, sky, sun and snow."

After that we sang and Johnny cut the tree down, turned the toboggan around, then tied the tree to it. We all walked out of the forest and when we reached the downhill area, Johnny told Andy and me to sit on the toboggan and slide down. We screamed in delight all the way down as Boots jumped and barked. At the bottom Johnny stopped and opened the orange juice and the Christmas cookies that mamom had baked and we had a rest time.

When we finally crossed the meadow and reached our house we came up to the front door, opened it and went into the kitchen by the big, old stove. We all had boots, woolen mittens, scarves and hats that mamom had made so were warm and comfortable outdoors but now took them off. We were all tired and thirsty. Mamom smiled as she looked out the window. She thanked God for life, for her children and that I had been saved. Johnny untied the tree, put it into the stand he had already made and we took it into the living room. How joyous we all were!

All of our Christmas tree ornaments were handmade from broken pieces of glass or china that were hung on strings. We decorated the tree and it sparkled in the sunlight.

The following morning we awakened to the aroma of bacon and coffee as mamom prepared papom's breakfast so he could go to work. We were very, very excited as tonight would be Christmas Eve. What a wonderful time. After breakfast mamom continued her cooking that would be primarily small pastries in honey and poppy seeds for our evening meal. Mamom managed to look at her children while she was cooking and smile at them with such love. The love of family will linger with me forever.

It was a bright, sunny day with many family members there. Finally mamom told us all to get cleaned up and to put on our best clothes for the special meal. At last we were called to the table and even more family members arrived just before we sat down to dinner. Mamom and papom had taught us with so much love of the beauty of Christmas Eve and the birthday of beloved Jesus. Papom said a special prayer for only Christmas Eve. We all enjoyed the pastries and many other traditional Hungarian foods. Oh, the dignity, the innocence, the unconditional love in that home. We were asked by papom to leave just a little on our plates as he would put it all together and take it to the animals to thank God for our blessings. The animals are blessed too.

We sang Christmas carols and little Andy and I could just smell, taste and feel the excitement. Later, with mamom's coaxing we changed into our handmade flannel pajamas. Mamom told us that tomorrow would be Christmas and Santa would bring a present for each of us, so we hurried to bed. I will never be able to forget that loveliness and innocence. "My dear God, you are so loved!"

On Christmas morning we were so excited we could hardly get through our breakfast with the delicious special pastries. Somehow we managed to eat and go into the living room to sit around the Christmas tree. Andy was the first to open his gift. It was a pair of tap dancing shoes. They were not new but were shined to a high gloss. Andy loved to tap dance and before any more gifts were opened he tap danced for us all. These shoes were symbolic of his life. He tap danced in school auditoriums and in many other places. Even as an adult he did his share of tap dancing.

My gift was in a huge box that was beautifully wrapped. It was an extremely large clock with a wonderful purpose to it.

Papom had made me special tools as I was always taking clocks apart and then putting them back together again. Such fun! It seemed my whole life as it continued was on a timer. Mamom said "Most girls would like a doll but Elu enjoys a clock because she likes to tinker." Of course I also had a big, wooden doll and kept taking it apart and putting it back together.

****

Growing up in the country was heavenly. There were fields and a meadow on our property as well as a large pine forest. Andy and I enjoyed our lives. I seemed to live to run and would run through the fields and think maybe I could fly, then stop suddenly and listen to the birds singing, trees whispering and leaves rustling in the breeze. I would walk up to a tree, put my arms around it and feel as though I felt the heartbeat of life in that tree. I would sometimes lie down in the meadow of fresh green grass and look up at the sky, clouds, hills and the warm sun next to a little, rippling brook. I would also run into the pine forest to the large circular area in the center to rest. There I would sit in the lotus position, without realizing it, and would somehow feel the American Indians and hear the chanting of those times.

It seemed like hours before I would return to the house. My mother would say, "Elu, have you been running in the forest again? Where are your shoes? Why don't you wear them?" She would ask me this same question many times over the years. To this day I do not like to wear shoes.

We had great fun sliding down the haystack in the barn but my father was always concerned about injuries because it was such a steep slide. One day I was outdoors and Johnny called me to come to the barn. I ran into the barn and papom said, "Elu, watch this cow giving birth." I did, then watched as the new calf stood on his wobbly legs. I remember saying, "How could this happen?"

At the time I started school I would run to a two-room schoolhouse about ten minutes away. The only difficult part for me was learning English. My older siblings were well educated and spoke it fluently but I had been speaking mostly Hungarian.

Andy was younger than I so when he started school sometimes he rode his tricycle. One day on the way to school Andy was pedaling and I was standing on the back as we went down a road that was hardly ever used by motorists. But that day a car came along slowly and we plowed right into it! We were unhurt but the news made the local newspaper and boy, did I "get it" from my parents! Since I was the older I certainly should have prevented that whole episode from happening.

****

A couple of years went by and life began to take on a new energy. Another event was coming -- Easter. Easter was an elegant, spiritual time. My mother prepared for weeks because she would carry large satchels of cream, cheese, butter and baked goods to our church convent and distribute them from our family. At times we would go into the church at sunset and mama would hold my hand. It was a very spiritual feeling. She would pray, "Thank you, God, for giving me back my child."

My mother would then start her cooking for us many days ahead and on Easter Sunday the best linen tablecloth and napkins would be on the table with the good china and it would seem to be a special meal before it even started. We had colored eggs as well as pastries with many wonderful aromas coming from the kitchen. Andy and I would run to the end of the driveway to watch for our brothers' car. Bill and our oldest brother, George, would always come with a lily plant for our mother, a bottle of wine for our father and presents for us. On some holidays they would come by train and we would meet them at the station.

It was never a problem in any way that my father was Lutheran and my mother was Catholic. In our house God was always a constant in our minds and hearts. Even sitting in front of the old, black stove in the kitchen, our mother and father talked about God's many gifts.

****

When I was eleven years old my brother, Bill, a professional barber and beautician visiting from Newburgh, NY, was giving me a haircut in the kitchen. The weather-beaten screen door was open and a thunderstorm was raging. A lightning bolt came in and struck the scissors in his hand and went from the scissors to my forehead. This has been told to me. I awakened in the arms of my mother. I remember her saying, "God has blessed you and called you two times. You have the gift." I did not know at the time what she meant. Maybe Jesus was recharging my battery!

****

My father was amazed at how I could fix the broken leg of a dog or cat or a cat's broken tail. Mama also taught me how to suture if necessary, how to put on a splint, and many other ways to help the animals when they were injured. Papom built me a little animal hospital in the back yard. It seemed to be used a great deal. Johnny built and painted a sign that said, "Helen's Animal Hospital." Eventually the neighbors brought some of their animals to my hospital.

I used Good Humor popsicle sticks for small animal splints at times. My father said I must have some of Thomas Edison in me.

One day my brother-in-law, Frank, who was a professor at Cornell University, was visiting. He was astounded to realize I was the "doctor" for the animal hospital. He said to my mother, "Mrs. Hudak, your daughter has such a gift, please let me pay for her tuition to Cornell University to study medicine when the time is right. I will pay all her expenses." My mother said, "Oh, no. God gave her a special gift – she knows – her life is planned way in advance. The college that she goes to is only of God." She never stopped teaching me. She said one day, "God sent you to me as a special gift. God is going to teach you and you must listen. I will help you along the way."

****

My energy was on a different level than that of my brothers and sisters. I was more sensitive to the crackling of leaves and twigs underfoot and the heart-beat of the trees. My awareness of beauty increased and sometimes I would cry because of the wonderful feeling. My mother would say, "Kicsi Elu, (Little Helen), you are my gift from God." My father would ask me if it was the right time to plant the corn or the peppers because he believed I knew.

Mamom taught me something very special which she realized my brothers and sisters would be unable to understand. She had an extremely beautiful cobalt blue glass bowl that she would fill with cold, fresh water from our well. The bowl was about twelve inches wide and when the bowl was filled she would show me how to ask questions into the bowl. Mamom took care of our basic healing needs but on rare occasions, if one of the children were ill she would ask, "Is it time to call the doctor?" A proper answer would come. One day I said to my mother after looking and communicating into the bowl, "Oh, mamom, Andy is going to fall and break his arm today!" Mamom told me to stay close to Andy in school to protect him but in spite of my efforts he did fall and, to my horror, did break his arm. I cried because I thought it was my fault.

I believe I was the only one of my siblings who realized the extent of our mother's mysticism, philosophy and intelligence. Sometimes I laugh and think she must have been a wizard and didn't know it. My parents never stopped teaching us. I would learn over the years from my mother how to run a home, raise children, cook, garden, do plumbing, laugh and sing.

At around twelve or thirteen years I could see some spirits. I had many visitors but mostly remember my grandfather and Aunt Mary coming to see me. I was very impressed with my grandfather's pure, white hair and small, white beard. He would touch me in the center of my forehead (the third eye). My Aunt Mary was my mother's sister and would always come holding the hand of her child who had died at age seven. She would come to me frequently when I was on my roll-up cot in the dining room as we did not have enough bedrooms for all the children at that time. She would say to me, "Don't be afraid."

I began to realize I was beginning to see things before they happened and yet was a normal teenager in many respects. As an example of my normality, my very favorite game was baseball. My pitching was excellent and my knuckle-ball was the best in the area. I still watch baseball at times.

My brothers and sisters were all beautiful, handsome and perfectly normal. Where did I come from? My life seemed to be taking on an essence of something so different it is hard to explain.

Chapter IV

ADULT STRUGGLES
AND HEALING

As we grew older life changed in many ways. One day Johnny and his fiancée took Roger Olsen and me to the movies. After that Roger and I dated for about a year, then decided to marry. My mother could not buy me a wedding gown so I found a picture of a gown in a magazine. Since I had learned to sew on an old pedal sewing machine, mamom bought fabric for $5.00 and I made the most beautiful wedding gown and veil one could ever see.

I turned 18 on February 7th. Our wedding was February 8th and February 9th Roger turned 20. An extremely bad blizzard struck in Connecticut on our wedding day so our planned honeymoon to New York City was canceled.

Roger and I had five children. During that time we moved several times, from a garage apartment to a small house and then to a larger one. I loved to plant flowers and one of my rock gardens is still there today.

One time when the doctor who had delivered all of our children was making a house call, as doctors did in those days, he was very concerned because his secretary was going to be leaving soon. I told him I was looking for a job and asked if I could be his secretary. We talked for a bit and thankfully, he said the job was mine.

This turned out to be the best job of my life. That fine doctor taught me the physiology of the body, how to suture, to assist at childbirth, how to sit with and comfort the dying and so much more. I had the ability to tell, when a patient walked into the office, what type of problem or problems that patient had. Of course I did not say anything but somehow he soon realized my abilities. At that time the diagnostic tests were not as advanced as they are today so sometimes, when there was some question as to what was wrong, he would have me come into his private office to discuss it with me. He also encouraged me to continue my education in night classes at the college close to his office. I was able to take psychology, philosophy, math and English, then do homework with my children. They certainly enjoyed that.

In November, 1963, I said to the doctor, "President Kennedy is going to be assassinated in three days. I was given the picture of a gun being fired from a bushy area, of President Kennedy being killed, his wife splattered with blood and another person in the car being severely injured." He said to me, "Helen, you have been watching too much television."

In three days the phone rang in the doctor's office and when I answered, doctor said, "Helen, have you heard the news yet today?" I had not so he told me not to turn it on, that he would be right in and wanted to talk to me. He arrived in just a few minutes, called me into his office and told me that President Kennedy had been assassinated. I fainted.

One day my family was enjoying a special day together. I was pregnant with my fifth child and being very cautious, wearing my sneakers, as my husband, Roger, and I were trout fishing in the Farmington River in Peoples State Forest in CT. I suddenly developed even more of an ability to see what was going to happen well before it occurred. I foresaw an automobile accident in which two people were killed. I felt extremely traumatized experiencing that awareness. I realized that sometimes it was going to be quite sad but I knew I must remain still. It was very difficult to do so. For the rest of my life I was able to see numerous incidents before they happened.

****

When my daughter Claudia was seven years old I had to go to the store. Claudia said to me, "Mommy, you shouldn't go out in the car today." If only I had recognized Claudia's abilities at that young age as my mother had recognized mine! I explained to her that we needed groceries but she said, "I don't want you to go in the car today!" I did go and consequently that day changed my life forever. I was driving a station wagon and was stopped at a red light when I looked in the rear-view mirror to see a car speeding toward mine. I had only time to step on the brake pedal so as not to go into another car when my car suddenly crunched up like an accordion, crushing my spine. A policeman pulled me out and called an ambulance which took me to Hartford Hospital. The woman driving the car that hit mine was drunk and had no insurance.

I spent many weeks in the hospital and over the years I required seven laminectomies (special spinal surgeries) so live in constant pain, even to this day. There is a lot of metal in my spine and I also suffered a great deal of muscle and nerve damage. Many of my back surgeries were done at a time when they were not as good as they are today so I have to live with those results. I prefer not to use narcotics so use acupressure to help.

****

Life changed as my children grew. One by one they left home for college or work. Our marriage ended so I then had to learn to live life without my husband. The discovery of yoga helped. I also learned meditation and, my favorite, mysticism. My mother called me a "wild Hungarian gypsy" and that was my greatest love.

I had within me the power of seeing and knowing telepathically and understanding the wonder of mysticism. I had a passion for God and wondering about the beauty, ecstasy and reality of our world. I also became quite an accomplished artist and did a great deal of portrait work. I paint even today. There are delightful etchings of my children, my friends, and my doctor.

Finally I met people who introduced me to the beauty of reiki, working with people with cancer, and many others. I remember all my clients. I remember especially Velita who was dying of cancer and came to my house in the pouring rain with her husband, Bill, also a beautiful soul. She looked like a little broken sparrow, who was crying and frightened. She said, "Oh, you're the dying lady." I said, "No, I'm the healing lady." We became good friends. I became her healer, housekeeper and cook at times. She stayed alive for 17 more years. It was a time of great learning. I learned about how cancer works and how it affects each person. My greatest challenge has been people with cancer. Velita used to salute me and call me "Captain," which made me laugh.

When Velita was in the hospital, near death, she never had any pain. She loved music so I played the radio music for her. When her doctor came in he asked her what she wanted and she said, "chocolate cake." He got it for her and then asked me to come into a semi-private room so he could ask me what I did that allowed her to be free of pain. I just said, "I don't do it. God works through me."

When Velita died I was asked to give the eulogy at her church. The music was beautiful with harp, violin and piano. There was a golden coffin and at one point during the eulogy I looked at the coffin. Because I sometimes see spirits, I saw Velita sitting on top of the coffin with her legs crossed. She saluted me as if to say, "Hi Captain!" For a moment I broke down before being able to continue.

The mind, like a river, winds restlessly, filled with energy. Sometimes roaring swiftly, sometimes deep and silent resting in the reservoir of stillness, then ultimately returning to the ocean in its constant cycle of collective consciousness.

The soul is the compelling force, aware of its infinity, working intimately with the mind and body. It is buffeted endlessly by the constant demands of the physical, the illusory fabrication of the mind and the dictatorial death fear of the ego.

This divinity within us brings us through a kaleidoscopic barrage of emotions from utter despair to bliss and enchantment. Like a grist mill, the soul takes the fruits of our consciousness, removes the pulp, refines, purifies and balances until we reach the perfection of godliness.

Finding that center, that balance, can take lifetime after lifetime to attain. Until we reach the center, until we accept the reality that all that we seek is within our very being, until we surrender to the God within us, we will wander endlessly in the worlds of illusion.

Helen Nelson 1983

Chapter V

COMING BACK FROM SURGERY

Early in 1975 I married a scientist, W. Nelson. Our home was in West Hartford, CT and I stopped doing healing work. I was busy being a wife and enjoyed decorating our beautiful house.

It was an April Sunday of that year as I looked around me and experienced the wonder of the beginning of a new spring. I had been home only two days from cardiac surgery at Hartford Hospital when my husband had to leave on a very important business trip. At the time I left the hospital my doctor told us both that I was not to be left alone at all for at least one week.

The soft fragrances of the season filled the air and should have brought a peace but I felt some apprehension as my husband was leaving and as we kissed goodby, I had the strangest feeling it might be the very last time I would see him.

The feeling didn't stay with me very long. After he left I walked around my lovely living room and touched all the pictures of my children, paintings that I loved, many things I had cherished for a long time and then realized I was not feeling very well. I began to experience some severe discomfort and knew immediately that it was wise for me to go upstairs and call my dear doctor. I got to the top of the stairs and was barely able to get into my bed but noticed an extremely bright light coming in the window. I tried to make myself comfortable, and as I reached for the telephone, everything stopped and there was nothing I could remember for a long time after that moment. I have to repeat here, this was April 1975. It is a day that will live in my memory for the rest of my life. I hope I can continue this with clarity and all of the emotion I experienced.

I felt nothing. I didn't realize that four days had come and gone. My husband called, my children called, but there was no response. While in Torrington my son, Brian, a beautiful, brilliant young man who is extremely telepathic, had the feeling he should drive quickly to my home, which he did. My car was in the driveway. He tried to open the door of the house but it was locked. He broke the door down, went upstairs to my bedroom and was appalled at what he saw. I suffer when I think of what a horrible memory it is for him to hold onto at times. He found that there was possibly some breath, some life and he immediately called the police, ambulance and my wonderful doctor. When they arrived at the house, I was not breathing. But my doctor, who was the Health Officer in West Hartford at the time, was convinced there was still some energy of life so I was rushed by ambulance to the hospital. There was nothing there that I can recall until one incredible moment which I will try to describe as vividly as I can remember.

I was taken to the emergency room. The first moment I can recall was that somehow I was above the table in the emergency room looking down as the medical staff worked on what appeared to be a lifeless body. I remember looking at it from another place above my body seeing that I, lying on the table, looked like a doll, a toy -- broken, shattered. Unbelievable, unbelievable, to realize that it was *my* body! Suddenly I felt around me and experienced what appeared to be a tremendous amount of electricity and it seemed that I was in another place. There was an echo -- a sound I will never forget. I encountered a space, a safe place, an exquisite place beyond description. The beauty, the beauty. The love, the tremendous, unconditional love that surrounded me! Somehow I knew that I had died. Was it heaven? I didn't know. Was God there? Yes, God was there. God was everything and everywhere. I was everything, I am everything and always will be. The music was so unbelievably beautiful that I don't think I will ever hear anything again in this life that even resembles what I heard at that time.

As I was in this exquisite place, I suddenly was between my mother and my father, who had both passed many years before. We communicated in Hungarian, the language I still love so much. Mamom and papom talked to me telepathically with love and compassion. Mamom told me I was in heaven with God, that I had died but could not stay -– I could not stay. Mamom reminded me of everything she taught me as a child, about God, about love -– unconditional love. Papom, mamom and I remembered our discussions when I was a child, always about God, the beauty of God, as it was in this place. I savored every instant of it. Mamom had me in her arms and said, "Elu, you MUST go back." I said, "No -– no more, I cannot. No more pain, no more hurt." But she said that I MUST go back! Papom told me that when I was a child at times I was the only one of their family sitting in the pew who was listening to his prayers to God. Then my father, in his so-called stern voice said, "Elunka, Elunka, you MUST go back. God has given you a precious gift and you MUST go back. God is always with you. You will communicate with the God in each person. Don't ever be afraid. There will be a time when there will be no more pain and life will be joyful. Your children, grandchildren and great-grandchildren will need you."

When I was told I had to go back because my family would need me, I begged God to please let me stay. Mamom and papom said, "Elu, you MUST go back. We love you, we are always with you, ALWAYS. You will remember this moment, this place, this love -- you will always remember but it will be difficult for you when you return as there will have to be much healing to your body."

During this time my spirit could experience the total beauty and ecstasy of God but back in the hospital emergency room there was a much different scene taking place. After much work by the doctors, part of which I had witnessed from above, I was officially pronounced dead. A sheet was placed over my body and I was wheeled across the operating room to the door.

Upon reaching the door, opening it and going through, the nurse who was accompanying my body suddenly noticed a nearly imperceptible slow rising and falling of the sheet over the area covering my nose and mouth. She cried, "She's breathing, she's breathing!" She rushed me back to the doctors, who somehow managed to stabilize me.

And now I have to go on to coming back to this world, coming back to this reality. And I wonder all the time, is this life really just a dream? Is it only a dream? Questions, questions, answers, answers, all the time. I was in the intensive care unit the first moment I opened my eyes -- and the first words that I spoke were, "I love you, I love you, I will always love you." That has never left me. When I did come back, all my children and my dear doctor were so happy.

I started a journey there in the ICU that I will never forget. As I looked around me I was in awe, despite all of the the noises from the respirator, the cardiac monitor and the other machines. I was aware of every person in that ICU and amazingly, each was surrounded by a beautiful circle of color, almost like a bright light of pink, blue, white, gold -- what did it mean? Each looked as if he or she were inside an egg and, as I was to learn years later, each color was the color of their spirit, their soul, their awareness. It was the aura of each of them but I didn't know this at that time. One nurse had a red aura and I was terrified of her. Today, if someone comes to me with a red aura I know something is wrong.

The love in that ICU was so great I just silently began to cry. My doctor said, "Helen, why are you crying?" But I could not talk, the tears just kept flowing. I was just in a state of awe. I realized that color would always stay with me and each person I would meet for the first time would be surrounded by that color, that aura, that light, which is what they are, which is what we are -- we are light. WE ARE THE LIGHT OF GOD. Oh, how beautiful to know this and to remember.

The days and the weeks that followed as I recovered were sometimes very sad, painful and frightening. I was totally incapable of holding a spoon or of using any part of my body. I had extensive paralysis and it meant months of therapy and awakening more each day – awakening. I continued to cry because I wanted to be free of pain and to be back with my parents where there was beauty and peace beyond anything I had ever known.

Sometime after being in the ICU I awoke to see a black nurse standing over me with her hands over my body. She touched me in many places that I would later learn were my energy centers, and as she completed her work I began to feel better. I felt very calm and had a healing sense of peace and tranquility. I felt within me a sense of love I had never felt before. She talked to me and told me I needed to stop crying and get better because I had much work to do. She gave me the strength and courage to keep going. After she left I knew I had the desire to go on. Something about me was different even though I could not tell what it was. The next day I asked to speak to the black nurse, as I wanted to thank her. I was told there was not a black nurse on staff that day or night and there had not been when I was admitted. When I told her of my experience she said, "Oh, that was just a dream." But it was not a dream -- I had been transformed and I knew it! Several years later I realized that same nurse was none other than my beloved Avatar, Sri Sathya Sai Baba, who had come to me in my time of great need! He is able to take on another form as He wishes as well as to relocate anywhere He is needed.

Then I was transferred to another special room where the seven patients were poor, lonely, elderly women preparing to die. It was so sad. I wanted to shout and to say, "Oh, if you only knew the beauty that is coming to you!" But they would not have heard me. Neither visitors nor clergymen came to that room which made it even more depressing. Only a nurse would come in now and then. All the patients were heavily sedated. Even the few flowers on some of the bed tables looked sad and despairing.

I looked at the women and slowly began to feel an energy and a passion -– an idea came into my being. I knew that all these poor, lonely women were waiting to go home but in spite of being there, something was happening to me -– I first realized that I had a purpose and thought someday I would be sitting next to and working with people like these, helping them to go home. I didn't know how or why but I knew that something in that room gave me such strength and such power because something in me awakened that I think I had hungered for all my life. For a while I had begun to feel like Sisyphus but now realized I was Helen and that I had been reborn physically and, above all, spiritually. I had been to hell and back. There is a heaven and a hell but it is in the consciousness of every living being. Something was reborn in me that I never knew existed.

I was there many weeks, but did recover with all the therapy and the love of that wonderful doctor. Every day he would come and say, "You're getting better, you're getting better, my Helen." And I was.

Then a peace began to settle within my body and soul and a hunger began in my being. Not for food nor water but for the sustenance of God. So overwhelming, so overwhelming because I still could not lift a finger. I knew that I must just be still -- be still, and I was. It was as if I had reached the top of the mountain. I looked at my children and an energy, a passion came into my being.

After weeks in that room I began to awaken. I could no longer be in there and bear to watch the women be carried out slowly one at a time so my doctor had me transferred to a new room where I was much happier!

****

Moving to a smaller unit that was a semi-private room in the hospital, looking out the window and seeing grass, trees, cars and the little flower garden right outside my window, was remarkable.

But then I went to look in the mirror, which I had not had access to for over two months. Upon looking at my reflection I immediately began sobbing uncontrollably! My doctor happened to walk in just at that moment, came over to me, took me by the shoulders and said, "What's the matter, Helen?" I responded by saying, "I'm not Helen anymore! These are not my eyes!" He hugged me and said, "Yes, you are still Helen -– you are, but you have been in a place so beautiful it is beyond description! You have come back and now you must get well. I will help you, I will help you." Oh, how he did. I am so grateful!

But something was VERY different about the appearance of my eyes. They were like deep, deep pools of light. Even my children would notice and comment on this. At the time I did not know that after my clinical death experience I was beginning to be in a gradual, new dimension of God. My awareness and reality were changing. I now had a new and intense desire to become well. Somehow my body began to develop some strength and I began to awaken. That was when my life started to change from the worldly to the divine.

It was a beautiful place, the continuing care unit, with many patients recovering. They would all come up to me and say, "What is that big light around you? May I touch you?" I thought it was so strange. Who am I, what am I? Then, after a while they would say, "Touch me, touch me." And I knew, yes, I knew, I had come back with the gift I always had, the gift of healing. My mother had been a natural healer and even though I had inherited some of that gift, now it was much stronger.

Slowly I recovered with physiotherapy, longing and desire. I worked with intensity and joy. Somehow now I knew I had a mission in this life, a purpose.

I remembered everything about Helen's life but from that time on the sky seemed a much richer blue and the world seemed more beautiful and new. From that time I thought and dressed differently. People looked different too. Now I could see people's disorders even stronger than before. For instance, I could see before if a person had cancer but now I could tell more about it. I was also to learn, much later, that much of cancer is the result of karma.

My doctor was astounded by my true desire to get well again. I knew at that time after weeks and months of recovery that my life was beginning anew. I knew that I was sent back to teach -- to teach how to love, to heal, and how to recognize the God in every human being, in every flower, in every tree, in every blade of grass. Oh my, what a gift I had. What a blessed gift to have. I remember asking the nurses to please take me in a wheelchair down to that little garden on the grounds of the hospital, and they did. And oh, to breathe fresh air again! I remember looking at that garden and the grass. I jumped, throwing myself out of the chair, onto the ground, kissed the earth, the grass, and I held up a few blades of grass to the nurses and said, "See this, this is God. See this flower? This is God. See that tree? That is God." Then I realized I should calm down so was taken back to my room. Memories, wisdom, joy -- pouring in.

What a wonderful journey I was again beginning in this place of healing. The love of people, oh God. My life after those weeks and months of therapy, of remembering, of hearing, of seeing, of knowing, sometimes I felt that I would just explode from all the beauty and the love. The knowing and the being, oh my, how thankful I am, how grateful I am, oh beloved Father.

When I came back into this new world it was painful, astounding and frightening. I saw the suffering, the pain, I saw the loneliness and the lack of wisdom, the lack of love and the incapacity to express love. Oh my, how can I do it Father, how can I do it? And God would always reveal the answer to me. To this day there's a special time when all the little problems are explained and shown to me.

So much happened after that. So much happened that I have to rest and begin the new journey in a little while......

Chapter VI

NEW BEGINNING

I was very fortunate to have a psychiatrist in the hospital who said to me, "Helen, what you have experienced has been experienced since the beginning of time so do not be afraid. Always think of it as a gift from God. You have been through so much, Helen, so much, but your strength, your love for your children, your love for life, and knowing deep within that you have a purpose, you have something to do, is bringing you through and we are here to help you." Sometimes he came two or three times a day. Oh, how he helped me! He explained to me about the people I had met who had undergone trauma, illness or surgery. He said I had what they called the telepathic ability to perceive and that there was much for me to do. He said, "Your doctor and I will help you get your life back on track and to find your way."

There was a young man who was studying to be a clergyman. He was still a student and many times we would walk the halls of the hospital at night as I was no longer able to sleep well. My mind was just racing and seeing things that I had never seen before. He was also a welcome part of my healing process.

****

I had been in the hospital over two months so I began to experience great anxiety and fear at leaving the comfortable, warm confines of the hospital -- with all the love, care, kindness and compassion that surrounded me. How could I continue my life? My husband seemed almost like a stranger to me now. He seemed irritated, as though I was wasting his time. As he helped me into the car and put in the few things that belonged to me, I could hear him grumbling about "all the time I am wasting."

Driving home was frightening to me. To be driving so fast with cars on either side. I looked out at the many, many houses scrambled here and there. I saw a large field of broken cars piled on top of each other. It was so frightening, so different. The sun did not seem as warm as I remembered it. The sky looked beautifully blue to me and I was somehow reassured as I could feel the gentle breeze coming in over the car window. Suddenly we were home and I was able to get out of the car by myself and walked with him to the door. As he opened it I walked into the house, astounded and frightened by the darkness. All the draperies were drawn, it was cold and I felt so uncomfortable, so frightened. I was confused. I didn't remember my home being like this. Now it just seemed big, empty and cold. All my beautiful plants had died and I fought to keep from crying. When the draperies were opened and the light came in I felt better. I sat in front of the fireplace looking at the pictures of my children. My husband stood in front of me and in a most demanding way said, "What's for supper?" I said, "I'm sorry, W., I don't think I can do that right now. You'll have to give me time to get used to being home and gaining some strength." So, in a very irritated way he said, "Well I'll just go get some Kentucky Fried Chicken," which he did. While he was gone I was able to bring myself back into a state of accepting where I was, who I was and why I was. I could not comprehend how my husband could neither understand nor comprehend what I had been through. It was very painful to me. I did not seem to belong here or anywhere anymore. There was a loneliness and hunger I could not understand. My husband did not understand my experience at all but my children were so loving, kind and helpful that slowly I began to come back into this life and this world.

Each day I was able to feel more comfortable and I returned to the reality that I was now living in. I wondered, kept wondering, who I really was. I remembered the awesome experience I had. I remembered my mother and father, the divine aspect, the stillness and serene beauty. I just wondered about it all.

After being home for a short time several clergymen from around the area would call to ask if they could come to talk to me about my experience. They were extremely interested and wanted to learn more. My husband, again, did not understand this at all and was quite annoyed by it.

That was just the beginning of my new adventure, my rebirth, my new life. Once I began to get my strength, thoughts and life back, a new world began for me. It was as if I had never seen the sky before or the flowers or my children. Oh God, it was so good. When God gives you a path, just follow. I followed. There was laughter, there was singing, music, love, joy and enlightenment beyond description. Enlightenment -– awakening to what this world really is. This world is an adventure after many adventures -– after many, many lifetimes. In each lifetime we have the ability, the wisdom and the love of God to direct and enlighten us. Each lifetime is a journey.

I don't see God in the same way I used to. Now I see God in every leaf, every bird, tree, blade of grass, every human being. The good, the bad and the ugly. It is all God. Some just need to reach higher levels. We are here to awaken those who cannot see -- those who are hungry for power or possession, money, or for a way to be recognized as great, and yet those are nothing. We are here to awaken to who we are. Each lifetime is a lifetime of growth and evolution. I can remember many of my lifetimes and am in awe.

My psychiatrist referred me to Dr. Kenneth Ring, a professor of psychology at the University of Connecticut, who was doing a study at the time on the clinical death experience. When Dr. Ring called I anxiously awaited his visit and when he came to my house I was quite comforted as we sat in front of the fireplace and talked and talked. Oh, Dr. Ring, your wonderful, gentle ways, delightful sense of humor, your comforting understanding as we talked, you consoled me and let me know that what I experienced was real and beautiful and that my life would be very different -- that I would be very different. I would have a different life, another world. I had experienced something so inspiring that it would be impossible for anyone to comprehend. I will never forget that day and that wonderful, beautiful Kenneth Ring opening a new door for me into a new life, a new reality. Oh, how exciting!

Dr. Ring asked that I come to his class in Storrs, CT and lecture to his students. Of course I was terrified at the thought of standing in front of an audience in a classroom but he was so consoling and always, with that wonderful sense of humor, that I began to feel very comfortable around him and enjoyed the experience. He also had me lecture in other universities and colleges.

The most beautiful experience of all was meeting Dr. Alvaro Bizziccari, Professor of Philosophy and Mysticism at the University of Connecticut. I was so honored to be asked by him to lecture in his class. Talk about shaking in your boots -- I always did and yet it was thrilling. We became close friends and he visited me frequently. Dr. Bizziccari was also a teacher of the beautiful "I AM" discourses, which I studied with great intensity. With Alvaro, who is still my lifelong friend, that period of my life was exciting and fascinating. Now, at this period of my life, I can say with the greatest conviction that his I AM teachings have intense meaning for me. He has since written a book, "DIALOGUES WITH MY GOD SELF Understanding the Law of Love" that is a masterpiece. At the end he explains the creative word "I Am." I have given out over 85 copies to friends all over the country.

I will skip here several months because I had moved to an apartment close to Saint Francis Hospital in Hartford after our marriage ended, and, by some miracle, I was then able to find a home in Storrs, CT. I was able to start a whole, new, beautiful life at this lovely home in the country with trees all around me and a cat that I adored, whose name was "Boobala." She was always in my lap, on my shoulders or on my feet when I slept at night. I was a very happy lady. It had what I called a "patchwork lawn" because I would plant one bag of grass seed at a time, only as I could afford to, until the whole lawn was gradually planted in patchwork.

I started my healing work there. I worked and studied hard. There would be days when I would awaken and be in such a state of pure beauty that I would just weep. One day everything was so brightly glistening that I was afraid I was losing my mind so I called my beloved Alvaro and he said, "Oh Helen, you are just experiencing a beautiful samadhi. Don't be afraid, just enjoy it." So he was not only my friend but my teacher.

While I was in Storrs Alvaro would visit me quite regularly. He would sit by my bookcase, look at the books I was reading and ask me questions. It was a period of great learning in my life.

Dr. Kenneth Ring would have wonderful social events at his home and I was always invited. He was so honored when I was there because I was always able to tell people about their past lives and things that astounded them. It was so beautiful. I will always treasure that time.

I remember listening to the lectures of Dr. Elisabeth Kubler Ross at the University of Connecticut. Eventually we became good friends and she became my teacher. She was a great lady who created the Hospice program and I learned so much from her. I remembered the time in the hospital when I was in the room with so many dying patients. I realized now that it was my time to learn how to sit with and comfort the dying. I was learning so much each day – a new life, a new world, a new reality. Oh, it was so good, so good.

With Kenneth Ring it was a wonderful journey. In fact our favorite song was Willie Nelson singing, "On the Road Again." We traveled everywhere -– Yale, Harvard, other schools and universities -- we were guests on many television programs such as Oprah, The Phil Donahue Show, Good Morning America and PM Magazine. One time while sitting in the waiting area of a television program in Boston, I think, I saw a man sitting in the same area with an aura which was the most beautiful I had ever seen. Finally he got up, came over to me and said, "Are you the lady who is doing the death and dying program?" I said, "Yes." He said, "I see you are in a lot of pain. May I touch you?" It was then I realized the man was the beautiful Rev. Billy Graham! I said, "Oh, yes." He really has it down -– he really knows what it is all about!

It was inspiring, delightful and entertaining, yet I knew that it would not be for me much longer. I knew that for me there was only one thing. My lifelong journey was to heal because I was given the gift that had now become so much stronger. I was also given more knowledge and wisdom and since that time I have continued to heal as much as I can. My life is so full, so filled with joy and love and with so much knowledge. Everything is a new journey, a new learning, a new discovery. I find of all the roads that lead to God -- Christianity, Buddhism, every philosophy -- there is only one way. There are many, many roads, but only one way to God and that is unconditional love. That is all I live with every day. I've gone through many difficult journeys, many periods of great despair and pain, a tremendous amount of surgery, great suffering. But somehow I found the strength, the power and the ability to survive. And now I pray always, God let me live, let me live. There is so much to teach, so much love to give. Please, Father, give me the strength. I thank God for my children, my wonderful children who have helped me constantly. All of them -- Roger, Brian, Claudia, Karen, Diane -- five awesome children, seven grandchildren and even great grandchildren but it still feels like my life is just beginning. Every day is a new beginning. There is so much, so much. My son, Brian, calls me "Reverend Mother" and that always makes me laugh.

Chapter VII

FAMILY LIFE
AND ENLIGHTENMENT

When my daughter, Karen, called to tell me she was having a baby and asked me to come and help while she worked, I left Storrs and moved to Torrington, CT to be with Karen and little Alyssa. It was familiar territory for me.

I found a lovely apartment, sun-filled, charming, close to a church. It was always so beautiful on Sundays as I could hear the church bells ringing.

I knew the moment I held that beautiful, little Alyssa in my arms, that it was what I was meant to do. Having a child to care for was part of my renewal process. I began a new life of healing work. I studied chakras, the meaning of colors, auras, more anatomy, disorders, despair. Slowly I received my reiki master certification, always learning throughout this time. To be around all my children was special for me.

I helped take care of Alyssa until she was in the 6th or 7th grade in school. She was like an extra appendage during her early years. She always sat by me. But when she no longer needed me so much it was time for me to move on and to start a new life again, to change. Love is such a mystery in so many ways.

I used to look in the mirror at those eyes of mine that seemed like deep, deep pools of light, that seemed to go into another divine place, another divine being that I realized I was becoming or had become and didn't know.

I found another place to live, a beautiful, little cozy apartment off a busy street in Torrington. I set up my healing room and started working. In between I took lessons in yoga and meditated constantly.

I was going into a higher dimension. One time there was an awesome moment when everything was crystal ecstasy. I called Alvaro who said, "Helen, you are now enlightened. You are totally awake."

Chapter VIII
THE WONDER OF INDIA
AND SRI SATHYA SAI BABA

One beautiful Indian lady, a cancer patient of mine, Rose Mancetta, and her husband, Nick, are beloved friends. Rose and Nick lived in NY and had heard about me so called to make an appointment. Rose was healed after several visits. I loved the Indian philosophy and psychology which they taught me. They were both so thrilled that Rose had been healed they offered me the gift of a trip to India. It was the most marvelous trip of my life and I will always be grateful to them. They live in North Carolina now and we are in touch by phone.

I took a plane to India and met my greatest teacher, Sri Sathya Sai Baba, the beautiful man in the orange robe. Meeting my beloved Sai Baba was the highlight of my journey. A whole month in India, listening to Him, seeing Him, being touched by Him at his ashram in Puttaparthi was ecstasy and I thought, "Oh, how I need this. How could God give me so much?" My beautiful Indian Avatar who is always with me. Yes, I have been given such gifts, rebirth and renewal and a completely different life with so much energy and special people included.

On the first full day, sitting in my room at the ashram, I said to myself, "I don't have anymore heart medication." Almost instantly there was a knock at the door and a sweet man said, "Mrs. Nelson, I understand you need some medication." I said, "How did you know that?" He said, "Oh, Swami knows everything." Then he had me give him my prescription and he took it to the pharmacy, had them fill it and brought my medication to me -– awesome!

I would like to explain here the meaning of the word, "darshan." It is the sight of a holy person or seeing the form of the Lord and receiving His blessing. The next morning as I was preparing to go to darshan, I nearly cried at the difficulty of putting on my new, elegant, blue sari. I remember thinking, "Oh dear, I wish I knew how to do this." There was again a knock at the door and a beautiful, young Indian girl said, "Mrs. Nelson, you need help with your sari." She taught me how to put it on and I felt so elegant and grateful when she had finished helping me. I thanked her and also thanked Swami for sending her to my door.

At 8:00 a.m. each day I would sit with hundreds of people to watch and listen to Sai Baba at darshan. The time went by magically. The only day I had been able to sit in the front row was the day there suddenly began a torrential rain in the middle of darshan. People immediately got up and ran for cover. I do not remember the rain lasting very long. Later there was a beautiful mandir built with the roof put over the whole large area for Sai Baba and the people who visited from all over the world. No more would rain disrupt anything that would take place there.

Upon my return from India, my home was filled with new energy, a new feeling and I had a new knowledge of meditation. It was really beyond words. As time went by I worked very hard learning to do hands-on healing. I had good teachers and worked with clients who had cancers, all kinds of disorders, pain, despair, agony, loneliness, and by the grace of God, was able to help them. I became quite active and had my own little healing facility. Each day was filled with wonder, love and joy. Our lives are beautiful and we have such potential.

It was an awakening for me to realize how meaningful our lives really are and that I must have the desire to meditate, study and restore a renewal of the beauty, to find the love and dedication that I must have to develop the art and wisdom of becoming a healer.

Following one of my last spinal surgeries the surgeon came in to see me. At that time I had a picture of Sri Sathya Sai Baba on my bed table in the hospital. He asked me about Him. Then he said, "Helen, I do not know your Avatar but I do know that it was not I who operated on you. I was there holding the instruments, but as soon as I began, a force took over my body, handling the instruments, and your surgery was completed in less than half the time I could ever have done it. It was a most *amazing* experience."

I never became too tired nor too sick to stop work and finally became a reiki master. Even though I already had an intuitive ability to heal, inherited from my mother, reiki helped me understand the balance of healing properly. It was a gift to be able to run my hands over a person from head to toe and be able to observe, intuitively, even the slightest disorder of the physical body. It is not, however, Helen doing this, but God, working through Helen, that is doing the healing, that is doing the talking, that is causing the laughter and the joy.

I have worked with people from all over the state and have done a lot of telephone work with people all over the country. I laugh at myself sometimes when I go to bed at night because it takes me thirty to forty minutes to say all my prayers.

THE WHISPER

Life

Is

A

Fleeting

Whisper

In

The

Night

BE STILL ------

LISTEN ------

Helen Lucas Nelson
8/94

Chapter IX
THE HEALING
MODALITIES OF LOVE

Father Aristide Bruni, a Catholic priest, helped me to understand and accept the reality of the new awareness and spirituality that had become so constant in my life. He gave a lecture forty years ago that knocked me off my feet! I have attended many more of his lectures over the years and listened to his beautiful Italian accent. We have remained good friends all that time and, together with a few others, have started a "Healing Modalities" program once a month. We started with nothing, but each healer has a different modality to work with. Every second Sunday we find a place where we can carry our massage tables for a few months and we have such a good experience. People come from all over and we have reiki, therapeutic touch and more. We talk and are like gypsies because we work for a few weeks or months then have to move on to find another place. So you see, I guess I am still a gypsy in my soul. But Father Bruni has been one of my teachers. The kindness, the love, the compassion that comes through that beautiful soul has given me the courage and the strength to continue on. He does so much healing work. I have the good fortune to sit with him once a month to talk and pray together.

All the back surgeries I have had are constant reminders to me that the body can be such a painful thing at times but I keep going. I understand that suffering is, in one way, part of the path to the divine. I have discovered the divinity of this life in this world. Each moment and each day is to me a reawakening of the divinity that resides in every human being. How is it possible to describe that in this world in which we live there is so much profound beauty, love and awakening? It is beyond description.

It seems I am not getting older, but younger, wiser. I have the knowledge that God is everywhere – in everyone and everything. I feel more joy, more beauty and, by the grace of God, have been given the ability to start painting and doing sculpture again, which I love passionately. It is like a new beginning.

I always taught my children about God. When Claudia was very young she pulled on my skirt one day and said, "Mommy, do think we are each a little speck of God?" Now Claudia Tar, she is a registered nurse living in North Carolina and is the recipient of my massage table. She has inherited all of my abilities and will put it to very good use.

Now I use a lot of visualization. Of course, not everyone is healed, depending upon the will of God. But I am still seeing people and get calls from all over the country. It is as though the person is lying on my table and I am working on them. At that moment I am not Helen at all. I am purely the mystery, the wonder and the beauty of God. I don't notice or feel anything – just an energy. I am spirit and I know that beloved God speaks through me. Oh, how I treasure that.

Cancer patients from thirty years ago are still calling me. Oh, how awesome! I have a very strong, deep awareness about cancer and I know there is more to come. I have only just begun.

There was great sadness at times such as when my brothers and sisters left this world. When my brother Andrew was very ill his wife and daughter were sitting in the hospital with him in the critical care unit when his wife asked if she could get anything for him. He said, "Yes, a chocolate ice cream cone." He was on a respirator and very close to death but she went quickly to the hospital kitchen, brought him one and handed it to him. He enjoyed just one taste when he suddenly said, "Oh, my God! Oh, my God! Oh, my God!" then died.

****

You cannot teach anyone to love. It has to come from the soul, the spirit, from God. Wellness also has to come from the soul, from the desire and the spirit. Healing to me is the most fascinating thing in the world. I want to leave as much knowledge as I can in this world before I decide to 'catch the bus' as we call it, to go home.

Time and time again I am reminded that no one dies – NO ONE DIES! We only transition. There is a beautiful, magnificent, unbelievably indescribable beauty that cannot be expressed in words. To this day the only way I can feel some of that ecstasy is through music.

There is so much in this world for everyone to learn, do and experience. How can I give hope to people who are despairing? We are reaching a place in our world at this time that is a stage of chaos. We have to make choices. We have to let go of the hunger for power -- the hunger for financial power, political power, and any indication of power. We have to understand that to survive in this world at this time we have to do only one thing –- love unconditionally –- LOVE UNCONDITIONALLY! Pay attention -– PAY ATTENTION! Our world is falling to pieces and only we, through the grace of God within us, can change it, can save it. I wake up every day asking for another day, another week, another year and life is good, life is good. I've learned to tolerate pain with the help of a wonderful new physician, a doctor who has been in practice for a long time and is one of the great ones.

****

On a spring day in 2011 my telephone rang. When I answered, a familiar, male voice with an Indian accent said, "Don't stop doing what you are doing. I love you." Then He hung up and I had a call shortly from the Sai Baba Center telling me that Sai Baba had left his body. He had died in India on Easter Sunday, 2011. Oh, the honor of His call!

BEYOND THE MIND

Beyond the mind, that bridge, that minute span that takes us in a split second from one level of consciousness to a plateau so beyond our greatest imaginings. That bridge is the moment when we become totally one with God or the Cosmic Consciousness.

We can spend a lifetime in meditation, contemplation, even resignation but somehow there has to be that perfect splitting, when the brain is totally stilled and the mind goes above and beyond all barriers.

For centuries, philosophers, mystics, yogis and great thinkers have tried every possible way to reach this point of infinite beauty and few have succeeded. Is it possible that the universe, this world we live in, had to be prepared and in one split instant we will reach samadhi, or universal consciousness, together? Are we as human beings separate or are we truly one nucleus vibrating together?

Will the positive be lifted in one instant and the consciousness in totality be raised to a higher vibration? Or will the negative be eliminated and the earth cleansed?

If we are the projected thoughts of God and He is still in the process of creating perfection, will the negative thoughts lose their forms and be dissipated?

Is Cosmic Consciousness still in the state of imperfection and developing rapidly to perfection?

Have we been so caught up in the element of time that we can not see that the universe is still in the process of creation?

Will, at the completion of perfection in the universe, all the dark or negative in the universe end?

When we all become of one mind, total harmony, will there be perfection and creation completed?

HELEN NELSON 1983

Chapter X

AWAKENING

It is as though God has sent companions into my life to help me on the way. About four years ago I met Lily and Frank Hsu from Taiwan. I call Frank my "Little Buddha" because he is more like Buddha than anyone I have ever known. He is a practiced man in acupuncture, acupressure and physical, spiritual, and psychological hands-on healing. He is totally enlightened! At that time I was very ill and he would come two or three times a day to help me get well, and I did. He is a miracle man. Lily is like a little butterfly, always flitting around bringing me the delicious food she cooks.

Frank looked for a house for over a year and many times I went with him. One day we found a house in poor condition on High Street in Torrington. I felt a very strong sense of emotion and said, "I think this is the house!" I had the emotion that the house number would be "2" but Frank said, the number is "11." I said, "What is 1 and 1?" Of course he said, "2." I remembered this house because it had been owned at one time by a Hungarian and Jewish couple to whom my mother had brought cheese when I was young. Frank bought the house and it has become "The Holy House" where he continues to do so much good work for many people.

I could go on and on with my story as there is so very much more. My five children, all adults now -- Karen, a brilliant, beautiful woman. I call her 'Little Angel' because she looks like one. Claudia, a nurse, following in my footsteps, all the way. Brian, a genius but doesn't know it yet, even when I keep telling him. He just says, "I haven't got time right now." My daughter, Diane, who had the courage, and I say courage, and wisdom to heal herself of breast cancer and wouldn't let me help. She said, "No, Mom, I'm going to do it myself -- you taught me how." She did and is cancer free. My son, Roger, with white hair and so handsome. When we are together sometimes people will come up and say, "What a beautiful brother and sister you are." Then Roger will say, "She's not my sister, she's my Mom!" Each one is like a beautiful mystery. Each is a lovely being experiencing God in a different way.

Sometimes I like to think of my adult children as a tree: Brian is the root system as he is very deep, very evolved. Roger is the trunk as he is strong but sometimes unbending. Claudia is very sturdy so is the branches and Diane is the leaves; colorful, changing, dancing, crying and laughing. Karen is the wind that blows through the branches and blows the leaves off the branches. She is waiting for the next spring.

Oh, awaken everyone, please awaken to who you are, to why you are, and to what you are. Are you compassionate?

When I see my seven grandchildren and my four great grandchildren, I feel God loves me very much to have given me this honor. I loved every moment of raising my family. All I can think is, we must -- we must -- save this world. There is only one way -- one way. There are many roads, many journeys, many teachers, but there is only one way to God -- unconditional love -- God is the teacher -- God is the vibration within all of us and within everything. Always, always, remember that.

As time goes by I feel younger with more joy and have been ordained as a minister of the Tao.

****

On July 23, 2015, Nancy and I had been working on this book for quite a while. On this particular day each of us had eaten only a light breakfast. Usually we stop for lunch but on this day we worked right through lunch time. All at once both of us felt a definite chill and I closed my eyes and said, "Baba's here!" (Sai Baba, as Jesus, is omnipresent). He said (telepathically) to me, "Remember, you are both still in human form so need to eat and rest." He also gave me a couple of other messages, then left. We had lunch, then visited until Nancy left for home before the commuter traffic.

The next morning I opened my eyes but wondered why everything looked very different. I had been blind in my left eye for many years but I covered my right eye and realized I could see clearly! When I went to see Dr. Neuwirth, he checked my eyesight and actually had tears in his eyes. He told me this was a miracle! [I can see clearly for distance now but still have great problems reading].

Chapter XI

CELEBRATIONS OF THE DIVINE

Andy and I played together all the time when we were young. Somehow we all grew up.

I have just had a magical dream. Oh, dear God, was that dream a gift from you? Is it you that I see –- that beautiful being constantly smiling, holding out your arms to me? Who is it? What is it? Of course it is Christmas and I am no longer a little girl. I am a woman and, oh my God, how did all this happen? Is this a life that is one instant in infinity? Is it possible that what I've had is only a dream? Was it a real experience? Have I lost my mind, my senses? No, I'm looking at my hands -– they are mine but older and still competent hands. I really think God has given me the greatest gift anyone could have on Christmas and that is a complete review of the life I am living and will continue to live.

Now I must arise, make a cup of coffee and sit down. This is extraordinary. I can remember every moment, feeling, touch, every light and every sound. Oh, my dear God, yes, it really was the birth of your beautiful son, Jesus, who was born last night. You are showing me that this life is a beautiful gift. There's been so much in that life. I must sit here and check myself to see that I am real.

I am alone here in my cozy little haven that I love so much. I will be celebrating today with my children and grandchildren and soon with my great grandchildren. When did all this happen? I am in my mid-eighties and have a son who is retired. Oh, my beloved God and my beloved Jesus. Thank you so much for this beautiful gift you have bestowed upon me. This gift of every moment, every memory from the time I was a little child. My beautiful, exciting life that I lived –- the love and beauty that I knew, the sadness I experienced. The wonder, the wonder of this life that I experienced. Oh, my God, my dear God, what a beautiful gift this is.

I think the coffee is ready now. I better have some and pull myself together before my children arrive. If they see me in this state they will think I have lost it. But they should know by now I have this ability to travel telepathically to the past and to the future, to experience the moment with gusto and so much gratitude. Oh, my Jesus, you are real, aren't you? But you give me such a hard time trying to paint you. Please help me.

I am, for once in my life, almost speechless. I must now make breakfast and pull myself together into the radiant Elu I have always been. It is going to be an awesome Christmas. My beloved God and Jesus, thank you for this gift. I will finish after breakfast.

Now, I hear the door and my handsome son, Roger, comes in with his lovely wife, Bonnie. I am always astounded when I see my children, especially Roger, my first born. Now he is retired. How is that possible? They greet me with "Merry Christmas, Mom – are you ready to go? Mom, how is it you always look so great? How long does it take you to put yourself together?" "It just takes a moment, honey, just a moment."

Now we are off. It is just a short drive to my daughter Karen's house in Torrington and as we pull in we are the first to arrive. Karen is always the hostess as she has the big house. We walk in with hugs and kisses. "Hey, Mom, you look great. Are you ready for a good party?" As usual I have my very special little love seat by the fireplace. As I sit down I look with awe at the beautiful, tall Christmas tree, all shining and bright, the wonderful aroma of Christmas and Karen's (tinkling) laugh. All the bustling begins to happen in the kitchen and as more and more people arrive I hear, "Hi mom, hi grandma." How delightful. I feel like the queen mother sitting there while one child at a time sits next to me. My beautiful Claudia, with a hug and kiss says, "How are you, mom?" Then my beautiful daughter, Diane, says, "Mom, you look better all the time. What are you doing, how do you do this?" That always cracks me up.

Then in comes my tall, handsome son, Brian. Attractive as the dickens and I am amazed at how fast this all seems to have happened. It seems as if only yesterday they were just babies. Now they are grown and somehow it seems an impossibility that I have raised these children, Roger, Claudia, Brian, Diane and Karen.

Then the grandchildren arrive one by one and I hear, "Hi grandma," over and over. It is beyond English words. "Oh, my God, how beautiful."

We all have a good time and then, suddenly, it is time for dinner. I am still sitting with one child or another. Dinner is delicious with everyone pitching in. We then sing carols and it is time to open presents. Somehow they always bring these gifts for me that are so lovely on this cheerful, warm day. I wish I could describe to them the dream, if it was a dream. Was it a dream? No, somehow I think I was taken back to that exquisite, heavenly sphere and had a brief communication with God and for one moment held that beautiful Jesus in my arms. That I had to keep to myself.

The day was lovely and then it was time for the family to depart. I was driven home by my son, Brian, and we laughed a lot. He came in with me, sat down and said, "Mom, how do you make this little place look so beautiful?" He gave me a big hug and kiss, then said, "Merry Christmas, Mom, you're pretty awesome. I love you."

****

Oh, God, I long so much to paint an aspect of you. I've been able to get the eyes, they came immediately, yet I must have at least six or eight coats of paint on the canvas already but I refuse to quit. I am so fortunate and so blessed. It has always seemed to me such a gift to be able to take a brush, pencil or charcoal and suddenly just let it happen. Ah, what a gift to be able to express myself in that way – in many ways. I want to take some time to see if I can finish the portrait of my beloved Jesus. Such radiance, such beauty, such love. I don't know, do other people experience this? I'm sure they do in their own way.

Looking back over my lifetime with my brothers and sisters, I remember on my fifteenth birthday Bela took me to New York to an opera. I wanted to be an opera singer but when I tried, with my low voice, mama would laugh. We may have had a large family but we had so much love. We grew our own food. We raised chickens, cows, goats and sheep. Today many children seem to have so little in comparison.

I want so much to thank my beloved God for all you have given me, the beauty I see around me and in everyone. I feel that sometimes it is beyond words and I cannot comprehend that this world is in chaos at this time. I cannot comprehend that a world of such beauty, expression, creativity and power still has wars, despair and unhappiness.

I hope that my children will remember all I have tried to tell them about my childhood, my evolutionary process as a human being and as a mother. Now I am writing away and waiting for another day when spirit will speak through me. Everything is possible. "Thank you, God, for all the gifts you have bestowed upon me. I love you."

It is as though I have climbed every mountain and had to come back down, then tried again and again. Climb that mountain, Elu, raise those children, teach them the power of love -- teach them the wisdom and unending love of God, to be aware of their divinity always. Oh, it was so good, yes. This book has been more than a story about my many fascinating, frightening and painful experiences. It is like music where you have to reach those high notes and then go down to the low notes to be profound music that almost makes everyone who hears it weep. I can never, as long as I am alive, be able to express my life, my adventures, my total unusual intense longing beyond description for the divine.

This year, on my birthday, my last surviving sibling, my sister, died. It was heartbreaking to me even though I know they are all living on another level. For a while I seemed to be alright but then I began to feel a depression and thought I had better do something quickly to help myself. When there was a free day for me and no one was coming to my home, I turned off the phone, settled into a state of quietness and went into a deep meditation. I am able to communicate with spirit so went to each of my brothers and sisters as well as my parents and spoke telepathically to each of them. When I came out of the meditation I felt as if I had entered a new state of happiness. Everything was normal again.

I can see the divine even now, at this moment, as I listen to the birds singing to me. The divine, as I smell the fir trees, the divine, as I can feel the sun, lovingly. I pray that in this book what people will recognize -— that what they long for all their lives -— is not "out there," outside of them. It is not in the stores or the mansions, it is not in any type of environment -- only in the acceptance and the awareness of the God within us -- US! We are blessed to be given this life, this time to experience what life is. It is not just playing, working, eating, laughing, and dancing. Oh no, every day there is something new, something beautiful, something profound that will come into your life and you will be startled at the beauty that you did not see before. Again and again God tries to awaken us, not only with words but with the wind, the sun, the rainbows, the clouds. Oh, and my beloved birds, dear Father, I thank you for this life and this opportunity to write about my experiences with the help of Nancy, her kindness, patience and her tired fingers typing away. I pray this may be a teaching lesson, maybe even a reward to someone who hungers for enlightenment. Someone who hungers for beauty or suffers from indescribable pain and loneliness. It is all within you -- the beauty, the love, the God, the essence of every living being on earth. Oh, awaken everyone, please -- awaken every day and take the time to stop and pray. Pray -- talk to God! You will be astounded when you feel and allow Him to answer. His love is unending -- indescribable and profound. Every day listen -- open your eyes and see beyond the superficial and see the awesome beauty that surrounds us.

One of my greatest joys now is sitting on the porch which has my bird feeder hanging very close to me and the wind chimes nearby also. The birds that have grown used to me being here and feeding them will come and sing to me. Sometimes they will land and stay a while on my hand or arm. Oh, how amazing this world is. How filled with emotion that it is almost impossible to describe it.

****

One very interesting thing is that for the past several days there have been no birds at the feeder. It is almost as if they know I will be moving soon to another town where I will have my own little house near the place my daughter, Karen, has moved. It will be overlooking a lake in Bristol, CT. I am so looking forward to this time. By the time this book is published I will been enjoying my new home.

<u>ILLUSIONS</u>

How magnificently
you set the stage,
as you
prepare me for
my final role.

Like a blazing star,
my earthly love
crescendos--
then--
slowly--
falls to dust.

My soul rings dry

and quiet pain

bleeds salty tears

as you my Lord, reach out

to set me free.

The last illusion

strips away,

and--

like thistle

drifting lightly,

rises to eternal skies

my soul at last finds peace.

Now my Lord!

Does my work begin?

Must I follow suit,

Be crucified

and suffer still the pains of man

or will this flame of mine

touch yours?

Direct me!

Use me as you will.

Helen Lucas Nelson

12/26/84

Chapter XII

HOPE

How can I possibly go from a state of divinity and ecstasy, an experience far beyond description? How can I possibly understand? How can I possibly expect anyone to understand the divine aspect in that heavenly realm?

Coming back to this earth has been painful and beyond description. I know the Helen that died and the Helen that came back are not the same person. Helen now has learned the beauty and magnificence of God, the beauty and the divinity of the angels and the spirits that surround us at all times. I have come back understanding totally that humility, forgiveness and unconditional love now fill my heart and my soul. I recognize that everyone, every human being on this earth, has a reason and a purpose for living. We must not die again and again before we recognize the divinity and the Godliness within us.

I have come back with one desire -- to love unconditionally. But I must also teach, heal and do anything within my power and my ability to awaken in others the God that dwells in each one of us.

Much of our world today is ill, and in total disarray -- chaotic -- lacking in love and conviction. What can we do? What can each of us do to change this world, this time, this place we call earth? We must love and give of ourselves. We do not have to die to awaken to who or why we are. We are all an aspect of the God that we worship. We must awaken! I beg you to awaken to who you are! Take the time, take the opportunity to be still and go deeply within your own being and experience the Godliness within you. This is an awesome world. It can be a beautiful one. It is as though chaos has taken over the earth. There is pain, suffering and illness everywhere. It is time <u>now</u> to stop and recognize the God within you that has the power and the love to change all that is existing now. It is time to allow the God within you to be the person you are.

I am so profoundly touched. I, as so many others, have died, have gone to the heavenly realm that is real -- very real -- exquisite beyond your comprehension yet it can be heaven here too!

What must we do to change all this chaos, the killing, the wars, the desire for power, for materialism? Everything and anything that is, can be and should be available to us. But we don't realize that we must learn unconditional love and humility before we can accept that Godliness that is all there for us.

Each day now is wondrous to me. I awaken constantly in severe pain but almost unaware of it most of the time because I have a purpose, an incentive that is such as I've never known in my life. I long mostly to heal those suffering from cancer and many disorders, suffering with pain and fear, loneliness and despair. How can I help? I can help, we can help first of all to love unconditionally, to awaken to the reality that God is in everyone, in everything and in every breath we take. Oh, what I saw, what I touched in that divine heavenly sphere is beyond description but I know now that the love I experienced and feel constantly is beyond anything I have ever known. I have been blessed in so many ways. By beautiful children, grandchildren and great grandchildren. We must teach our families the importance of love, dignity, prayer and the importance of having the awareness of the

God in everyone. We have much work to do. We have an earth that is sick, also poisoned, destroyed almost beyond repair from the neglect and disturbances that were unnecessary. My hunger is <u>so</u> intense. I awaken each morning with a tremendous desire to help change the world. I see people suffering from a lack of divine realization, having somewhere, somehow along the way lost their communication with the God that is within their own being and within every other being.

Oh, what a beautiful world this can be. God has given us tremendous abilities, wisdom and ability to love unconditionally. We are <u>so</u> loved by the Divine. I am so filled with that light. I cannot even explain because I have never known such joy and such peace before. There was always love in my home, my family, in my childhood. There has never been a time when there has been no love.

I long so much to awaken everyone. We can do it all together. We can make this into a world of the divine that is surrounding us. We can grow and evolve as it continues to surround us. We have a responsibility to heal the world, to bring it all back into a divine state of equanimity, Godliness and unconditional love.

God, oh yes, God is real. God is more real than you can comprehend.

Oh, embrace your own beauty. Embrace the God within you. Open your heart, open your soul. Together we can create a world of ecstasy and divinity.

I beg everyone who hears my words to look in the mirror and see who you are. You will be astounded if you continue looking; you will recognize you are part of the whole which is only one. Let's give it a try, let's awaken -- open your heart, open your mind, open your soul. Open your arms!

I love you all, my dear friends. Help me, help God to rebuild this beautiful earth.

I thank you with all my heart and soul. Touch the God within you, reach the God within you. You will be so filled with joy it will be almost unbearable. Do it today!

God bless you, God keep you, God loves you. Let's make it a beautiful tomorrow, tomorrow and tomorrow.

HOW WILL HE COME

HOW WILL YOU COME MY LORD

With thundering oratory

in flaming burnished robes …...

Footsteps rending past the hungry throngs.

Will the earth tremble as the mountains

slide from their stately guardian posts?

The skies pouring forth with lashing gale

tearing the deeply bedded roots.

Will the mountains surge to reach the stars

and waters spew abandoned waves

as they cleave new horizons?

Will it be vengeance

or cleansing as you lift your mighty sword?

HOW WILL YOU COME MY LORD

Will it be as softly as the morning mist

that hugs the earth in sparkling hues

Or in evenings silent sleep …...

Will thou touch my lips with trembling fingers

hoping for remembrance?

Might you leave lonely footprints in the sea washed sand

hoping that we will follow

unquestioningly ….

HOW WILL YOU COME MY LORD

WHEN WILL YOU COME?......

Soon …... Helen Lucas Nelson 1982

Printed in the United States
By Bookmasters